One Special

The Story of Andatu

Written and illustrated by the fifth graders of P.S. 107 John W. Kimball Learning Center

Foreword

The P.S. 107 John W. Kimball Learning Center, an elementary school in Park Slope, Brooklyn, is far from the jungles and grasslands where Andatu and most of the world's remaining rhinos live. Yet in 2012, some school parents started the PTA committee Beast Relief, to teach students about the need for wildlife conservation and to inspire a love of animals. Particularly concerned about the rampant poaching of rhinos, we encouraged students to embrace their cause through spare-change drives, art and video projects.

For this book, we focused on Andatu because his story is hopeful. Though fewer than 200 Sumatran rhinos remain alive, he is the only one ever born in captivity in Indonesia, and may play a vital role in his species' future. We invited the fifth graders to put themselves literally in his hooves. Using research materials provided by the International Rhino Foundation, the students wrote from his point of view. We then re-assembled their accounts into a narrative. The students illustrated sections of the book. The project, which spanned the school year, involved the entire fifth grade.

We hope this book will inspire other students and schools to join the fight to save rhinos and other endangered wildlife.

- P.S. 107 Beast Relief

Hi,
my name is
Andatu.

I'm a Sumatran rhino. I'm covered with a light layer of hair. Out of the five different species of rhino, we are the only ones with hair all over our body. Cool, huh? We are also the smallest.

Javan
Rhinoceros

White
Rhinoceros

Sumatran
Rhinoceros

Indian
Rhinoceros

Black
Rhinoceros

I don't have much of a horn yet, but I will in a few years. You see, rhinos are born without a horn but as we grow, our horn grows with us.

4ft

3ft

2ft

1ft

My mom's name is Ratu and my dad's is Andalas. My name is my parents' combined. Think about it. Andalas + Ratu = Andatu. It only took me a year to figure that one out! Smart, huh?

Andalas + Ratu = Me!

Andatu. I like the ring of it.

In the local language, it means `gift from god.'

I live in a place called the Way Kambas rhino sanctuary, which supports us rhinos so that we are happy and good to go. Five of us live at my place. Me, my mama Ratu, my daddy Andalas and two others, Rosa and Bina.

When my mom gave birth to me, I symbolized the hope of the new Sumatrans. I was called the "Miracle Baby." Rhino babies are born a lot in Africa and India. But I was the first Sumatran rhino to ever be born in captivity in Indonesia. That makes me one special rhino.

Indonesia

Like all rhinos, I and the other Sumatrans are in trouble. We are critically endangered. There's only 100 to 200 of us IN THE WORLD. We are being killed by people. Shocking, right?

When there are so few of us, it's hard to find friends to play with. This is sad to me.

So I'm here to tell you about my life and ask for your help.

My mom was born in the wild. When she was little, some people mistook her for a large pig and tried to kill her. Ouch! That must have hurt her heart! My mommy left them in the dust. The park rangers rescued her and put her in the rhino sanctuary.

The Cincinnati Zoo, which is very far away from here, is where my daddy was born and grew up. My grandparents Ipuh and Emi were taken in there to save my species.

My grandma got pregnant five times but none of her babies ever made it... until Daddy. He was the first Sumatran rhino born in 112 years. At least, in captivity. Everyone was thrilled!

My father Andalas was small, the size of a doggy, when he was born. He didn't have a horn yet. But he was happy. He loved to snuggle with my grandmother Emi. He nursed every hour and put on two-and-a-half pounds a day. Sometimes I try to act like him and see what being that BIG must feel like.

My daddy had many friends at the zoo. In 2009, they moved him to Indonesia (he was brave to go on the journey) where he met my mom. They fell in love. Then, I was born.

On June 23, 2012, I entered the world with a thump. A three foot drop down to earth didn't faze me at all. It was nighttime. Bright lights from flashlights blinded me as I slowly opened my eyes to the world. Well, a small part of it.

I gazed around this mysterious place. A huge hairy thing towered above me. "Who's that?" I whispered, my eyes wide open. "Andatu, that's your mom!" A voice said. My mom nudged me with her horn as if to say, `Go on.' Slowly, I took a step.

Ever since birth, I loved to eat. Eat, eat, eat! I nursed from my mom every day. I ate delicious leaves from the jungle, sweet potatoes, just about anything.

I ate so much,
in a year I went
from 60 pounds at
birth to over 900 pounds.

I enjoy wallowing almost as much as I love eating. Mud baths are what I enjoy most: the feeling of that rich, gooey, lovely filth all over me. I also enjoy water: sitting, splashing, bathing. When the sun is angry, it beats like flames on my back. Luckily, the fresh tropical trees guard me from the sun's harm.

Then there's animal watching. There are owls who are awake at night and make noises when I'm trying to go to sleep. I see snakes slithering around the sanctuary, spiders bouncing, ants marching, birds flying, monkeys howling and, of course, people. Since I am around them so often, I am not scared and don't mind if they try to touch me.

Three keepers named Gocek, Giano and Iswanto keep me and my mom clean and healthy. They feed me, wash me, inspect my feet and weigh me. Dr. Dedi Candra is the veterinarian for all of us rhinos. He is a rhino expert and decides what foods we will eat. If I'm sick, he gives me medicine.

There's only one thing I'm scared of. It's called a poacher – people who shoot rhinos for our horns. I know, right! Who would do such a thing? Well, some people think that rhino horn cures cancer, but really it doesn't. Our horns are made from the same thing you humans call fingernails and hair. So if they want to cure themselves that way, why don't they just bite their nails and eat their hair? Why kill us for the same thing?

Many of my relatives have been killed and I'm tired and upset about it. There are very few of us left. We Sumatrans are related to woolly mammoths, and they're extinct. We do NOT want to end up like them.

My mom says she once saw some poachers. As I heard the story, I spun around and around, looking for any. Thankfully, many caring wildlife conservationists have been taking us in, and nurturing us safe from poachers. I'm grateful for that.

Rhino protection units are there to make sure no poachers are lurking around. They specialize in unhinging traps and snares. They take shifts, about 15 days per month, to monitor the area. My mom says they will help us stay out of trouble.

Today, my eyes are filled with surprise. A cake made out of grain was before me. Banana coated it. Berries decorated it and leaves surrounded the amazing structure. "Happy birthday, Andatu!" My keepers said. I licked the cake and snarfed bits of berries into my mouth. I was making a mess but I didn't care. It was my birthday.

As I gobbled it up, my mama stood next to me. Her eyes were shining. I love my mom because she has stayed with me all the time.

I like watching the sun go down. It winds down the day, the way I am winding down my story.

Now is the time to help me, mom, dad and every other rhino that's in danger. You can help by celebrating Cinco de Rhino, Bowling for Rhinos or you can even adopt a rhino like me. In the end, I want our population to increase. I want more friends.

I hope that I can be a superhero rhino,
who helps rhinos around the world.

Thanks for listening.

Lisa Anik
Owen Anna Katy
Ava Joshua Ella Tess
Matthew Isaac Jonah
Max Valerie J David Ellis
Liam Jovon James Jese
Eli Catherine Phoebie Mateo
John Colin Socrale Brianna Vicktorya
William Annabelle Sasha Ruby
Siena Eli Lilly Thomas Dominique Nicky Oliver
Aidan Da Me Brian Mesta Oscar
Jonathan JohnGus David Lulu Janibel
Aaron Owen Cameron Sylvie Mika Eliza
Enzo Jessica Alex Drew Marina Jayda
Mairin DrewAmanda Aniella Jonah
Arman Madison Finnegan Gaia
Sophia EvA Samson Holly
Horace Aliya Isabella
Abigail Makai Galie Iason
Nicholas Ava Naomi
Cornell

Acknowledgements

The Beast Relief committee would like to acknowledge the International Rhino Foundation, which provided research material, photographs and essential guidance. The Cincinnati Zoo shared photographs of Andatu's extended family. Eve Litwack, P.S. 107's inspiring principal, encouraged this project and helped us overcome logistical challenges. Chris Eastland, co-founder of ZooBorns, played a central role in designing and formatting the book. Fifth-grade teachers Dominique Freda, Michael Carlson, Sarah Hunt and Amanda Porzse helped bring this project to all 84 fifth graders.

And of course, without our talented fifth graders, there would be no book.

www.rhinos.org   www.ps107.org/beastrelief

Made in the USA
Lexington, KY
16 May 2014